Original title:
Paths of Peonies

Copyright © 2025 Creative Arts Management OÜ
All rights reserved.

Author: Elias Montgomery
ISBN HARDBACK: 978-1-80566-651-6
ISBN PAPERBACK: 978-1-80566-936-4

Trails of Color and Light

In a garden where colors shout,
I tripped on a bloom, now that's no doubt!
Roses laughed, daisies gave a cheer,
I'm the clumsiest gardener here!

Leaves twirled like dancers in a show,
I waved back, and forgot where to go.
A sunflower winked, I felt quite bright,
Flipped upside down, what a silly sight!

Wandering Among Blooming Hues

With each bloom, I try to pose,
But bees took my hat, oh what a rose!
A tulip chuckled, said, 'Get in line!'
I said, 'Fine! Just don't make me dine!'

Lettuce giggled as I stepped near,
Told me to frolic without any fear.
The violets joined in a singing spree,
While I danced like a bee—oh surely not me!

Echoes in a Sea of Petals

Amidst petals, I took a leap,
Landed in buttercups, oh what a heap!
Petals whispered secrets of the day,
"Keep your shoes on, or walk our way!"

Winds play tricks, as flowers joke,
A daffodil teased, 'You need to poke!'
Echoes of laughter floated around,
As I stumbled upon soft flower ground.

Serene Walks in Velvet Gardens

In gardens soft as whispers, I twirl,
Where pickles bloom? Just give them a whirl!
A snail wore glasses, said, "Take it slow,"
While crickets chimed in with their own show.

Petunias dressed up, held a grand ball,
Invited me over but I took a fall!
With petals like pillows, I softly land,
As bees laugh at my clumsy stand.

Tapestry of Floral Fantasies

In a garden of giggles, blooms take flight,
Dancing daisies brandish, oh what a sight!
Roses recount tales of their dramatic flair,
While lilies whisper secrets on the warm air.

Tulips wear top hats, vied for a crown,
Sunflowers laugh, never wearing a frown.
Marigolds sing songs, their voices so bold,
As petals paint laughter in colors untold.

A Pilgrimage of Colorful Essence

Bumblebees chuckle, trailing a tune,
While butterflies waltz beneath the bright moon.
Petunias perform, a lively ballet,
As violets plot pranks in the light of day.

A daffodil juggles with a cheeky grin,
Swaying to rhythms, oh where to begin!
With every sweet scent that dances the air,
Laughter blossoms, joy is everywhere.

Stories Written in Scented Valleys

In the valley of scents, a tale is spun,
Where herbs groove at dusk just for fun.
Jasmine and mint share hilarious lore,
As gardeners chuckle, needing much more.

Chives play charades, tickling the breeze,
While wildflowers plot tricks, oh such mischief they tease!
Each petal a story, each fragrance a line,
In a riot of colors, they joyfully shine.

Impression by the Edge of Blooms

At the edge of the blooms, laughter grows wide,
Funny lilies giggle, all giddy inside.
A trail of bright petals leads off to the side,
Where daisies conspire, in mischief they guide.

Each blossom a joker, each color a jest,
In this garden of humor, they dance and they rest.
The sun gives a wink, with warmth on their cheeks,
As nature's own comedians giggle for weeks.

Beyond the Garden Gate

In the garden, where flowers play,
Little bees dance in disarray.
Rabbit hops with quite a flair,
Chasing butterflies in the air.

Sunflowers grin with sunny glee,
A hedgehog hums a symphony.
Daisies gossip, oh so sweet,
While daisies wiggle in their seat.

Ladybugs wear their little spots,
While grasshoppers give silly plots.
The lilies laugh in shades of white,
Underneath the moonlight bright.

Through petals soft, the breeze does sneak,
With charming scents, it loves to peek.
In this space, pure joy does bloom,
Where laughter fills each sunny room.

The Allure of Vivid Petals

Roses wear their rosy cheeks,
While tulips flaunt their perfect peaks.
Petals flutter, what a sight,
Color fights for who's more bright!

In this plot of blooming fun,
Bees and flowers all just run.
Peacocks strut with all their grace,
Trying hard to win this race.

Carnations argue, red or pink,
While violets cheer and wink.
With a giggle, bloom ignites,
Creating joy in sunny heights.

Every sprout has something to share,
A joke, a laugh, without a care.
With nature's quirks, we lose the frown,
In this riot of color gown!

Whispers of Blooming Trails

Hummingbirds sing their raucous song,
As daisies sway all day long.
With their heads held high and bright,
They tease the sun; oh, what a sight!

The grass tickles with playful glee,
While ants march in a conga spree.
Squirrels chase beneath the trees,
Whispering secrets in the breeze.

Butterflies wiggle, strut, and sway,
Each petal holds a chance to play.
In this garden, joy prevails,
As laughter rides on fragrant trails.

Every bloom shares quirky tales,
Of wiggly worms and silly snails.
Life unfolds in splendid hues,
In giggles made of morning dew.

Garden of Fragrant Footsteps

In the garden, shoes take flight,
Stepping blooms in sheer delight.
With petals soft beneath our toes,
What laughter flows, everybody knows!

Fluffy clouds in a dance parade,
Whispering secrets, they never fade.
Slips and trips among the greens,
Oh, the joy in all these scenes!

From daisies bright to tulips tall,
Each step brings out a chuckle's call.
Sunsets clad in rosy shades,
Tickling senses, bright charades!

In this garden of fragrant whims,
Nature hums its beautiful hymns.
As we frolic through this space,
Every mumble finds its place.

Light and Shade of Floral Whisperings

In gardens where the daisies giggle,
And roses blush from every wiggle,
A bee with swagger, full of cheer,
Swaps tales of pollen in our ear.

Bright sunbeams sneak through leafy bars,
While shadows dance like little stars,
A dandelion dons a crown,
Proclaiming he won't ever frown.

The lilies plot some gentle pranks,
As tulips form their noble ranks,
They tease the weeds that try to boast,
And all join in a fragrant roast.

With laughter soft as petal's sigh,
The blooms concoct their wildest lie,
In whispers sweet beneath the sun,
Each moment shared, a blooming pun.

The Allure of Hidden Gardens

Beyond the gate, where secrets sleep,
The blooms conspire, their secrets keep,
A lilac knows a gossipy tale,
While honeysuckle drapes like a veil.

The violets wear conspirator's hats,
While daisies exchange silly spats,
With every hedge and every turn,
New tricks from every plant we learn.

A squirrel sneaks a berry stash,
While roses giggle at the crash,
The pond reflects the sun's bright kiss,
And lily pads swim in blissful bliss.

In hidden nooks, the flora tease,
A parade of colors in the breeze,
With laughter echoing through the night,
In gardens where the heart takes flight.

Hues of Remembered Paths

The trails we stroll are painted bright,
With petals dancing, pure delight,
A poppy twirls, a daisy spins,
While tulips wink at silly grins.

Each step reveals a new surprise,
As sunflowers play peek-a-boo eyes,
A carpet of colors underfoot,
With laughter wrapped in every root.

In every bend, a memory blooms,
Through trials, joy, and silly dooms,
The marigold plans its next charade,
While ferns join in the grand parade.

A path adorned with giggling blooms,
In vibrant hues, our spirit zooms,
With every chuckle, every cheer,
Their whispered joys are ever near.

The Landscape of Kindred Blooms

In gardens where giggles do play,
Flowers tumble in a bright ballet.
Ladybugs sport their polka-dot spree,
Dancing while bees hum their sweet decree.

Petals hold secrets, whispers so loud,
Telling the tales of a merry crowd.
With daisy chains twinkling in the breeze,
They gossip about the world's strange Knees.

A sunflower winks, what a cheeky sight,
As tulips debate who's the fairest tonight.
Laughter erupts, echoing through the air,
In this whimsical realm, no one has a care.

Martyred Petals Under the Stars

Under a moon that's gone a bit round,
Petals plot mischief without a sound.
Roses tug at the arms of night,
While violets play hide and seek in the light.

Their colors explode like confetti in dreams,
As daisies construct their unworldly schemes.
Pansies wear masks, trying to blend,
As night critters laugh at how they pretend.

But oh, what a riot when morning arrives,
Unruly blooms stubbornly strive.
A comical battle 'tween flower and sprout,
As humans obliviously wander about.

A Sojourn Through Herbal Dreams

In fields where thyme tickles the toes,
Basil and parsley strike silly poses.
Mint tries to steal every show that it sees,
While chives laugh softly with the summer breeze.

Cilantro makes friends with all who will stay,
Sharing tales of taste in a funky bouquet.
With each fragrant twist, laughter will soar,
As fennel stands tall, just begging for more.

Lavender giggles, a calming perfume,
While sage plots a heist on the sun's warm bloom.
Every herb's got a joke, a quirk, a line,
In the garden of dreams, where all things align.

Flickers of Color in the Moonlight

At dusk, when the world's at its best,
A riot of colors puts patience to test.
Lilies in laughter, they twirl and sway,
Under the silvered glimmers of play.

Irises gossip with lilacs in tow,
While peonies blush, stealing the show.
Each flicker a chuckle, each shade a grin,
As the stars sparkle back, letting the fun begin.

Petals plot pranks in the cool night air,
Swapping their petals, a colorful flair.
With every chuckle shared 'neath the bright sight,
They bask in the humor of the warm night light.

The Beauty of Wandering Blooms

In gardens wide, I trip on weeds,
A dance with dandelions, so comical indeed.
The roses laugh as I tumble down,
They whisper jokes, the floral crown.

With petals swirling, I spin and prance,
A tulip twirls, inviting a chance.
I slip on a bloom and fall with flair,
The violets giggle with petals in the air.

As bees buzz by, I wave hello,
They buzz around in a lively show.
In this floral circus, I find my way,
With blooms as my buddies, we frolic and play.

So here's to blossoms that lightly tease,
In this garden of laughter, I'm always at ease.
With every stumble and joyful cheer,
The beauty of wandering brings me near.

Petals and Promises Along the Way

With petals bright, I wander and roam,
Each flower whispers, "Make us your home!"
I promise to dance with a lilac spry,
While daisies join in from the nearby sky.

A tulip teases, "Come take a chance!"
In this vibrant field, there's room for a dance.
The sunflowers wink as I trip in the grass,
Their sunny smiles help the moments pass.

Around the bend, a lilting breeze,
Picks up my hat and sets my heart at ease.
I chase the petals that swirl in delight,
With giggles and glances, we take flight.

With promises made beneath the blue sky,
I vow to laugh as the day goes by.
For in moments like these, I find my play,
In the blooms and breezes, come what may!

The Eternal Quest for Floral Serenity

On quest for peace, I wander with glee,
But every step leads to a bumblebee.
They think I'm sweet, their buzzing parade,
As I dodge and weave in a floral charade.

The peonies giggle, their petals aflutter,
Gossiping secrets as I stumble in clutter.
"Is that a new hat?" they whisper with glee,
I nod and reply, "Just a flower-loving spree!"

A patch of roses, so finely arranged,
In their deep colors, my focus is changed.
Each thorn a reminder to lighten my stride,
In this playful garden, I'll take it all in pride.

So here's to the quest for that tranquil bliss,
Amidst laughs and blooms, it's a sweetened kiss.
With every step, I embrace the fun,
In a world of flowers, I've already won!

Echoes of Spring Upon the Earth

As springtime dances, I join in the fun,
With petals a-fluttering, I leap and run.
The echoes of laughter, so sweet and light,
As blossoms bloom in a colorful sight.

Each step through fields feels a bit like play,
With hostas as pillows where I dream away.
A poppy shoots up, "What's your name, dear friend?"
"I'm just here for laughter, let the joy extend!"

With sunbeams swirling like cheerful balloons,
I sway with the flowers, singing silly tunes.
The daisies nod as I skip to and fro,
In this floral playground, my spirits grow.

So raise your voice, let your joy outburst,
In these echoing blooms, I've quenched my thirst.
For spring brings laughter, so pure and clear,
With every flower giggle, I hold them near.

Rays of Hope Amid Dewy Petals

In the garden where we play,
Dewdrops giggle, bright as day.
Bees wear hats that make them swoon,
The flowers dance and sing a tune.

Sunlight sprinkles joyful grins,
While worms are flinging silly spins.
A butterfly with silly flair,
Lands on noses, unaware!

The daisies plot a grand parade,
While tulips giggle, unafraid.
A rogue snail sneaks a quick peek,
Then swiftly hides, becoming meek.

But when the rain begins to fall,
The petals slip, they trip, then stall.
Laughter echoes, joy ignites,
In our garden's funny sights!

Trails of Colorful Solitude

On a path of petals bright,
A lone giraffe takes flight.
It prances in a flower hat,
And whispers secrets to a cat.

The lilies burst into a laugh,
When daisies try their best to dance.
A butterfly trips over its wings,
While nature cheers and joyfully sings.

The sun plays peek-a-boo at noon,
As otters steal a bright balloon.
A parade of ants march in line,
With tiny drums and axes divine.

Yet under the shade, all alone,
A cactus pricks its woeful tone.
"Hey guys, why don't you stop and chat?"
But flowers giggle, "We'll call you back!"

Traces of Nature's Gentle Thorns

In a rose bush, oh what fun,
Thorns complain when battles run.
"Why must we poke?" they sadly sigh,
"Can't we hug like clouds up high?"

The prickly pins are feeling shy,
While bees mock them as they fly.
"Join the party, might you dare?"
"No thanks," say thorns, "we'd rather wear!"

A butterfly stumbles on a thorn,
And curses softly, getting worn.
"Hey flower friends, don't you agree,
These prickly pals just can't be free?"

But thorns have stories, brave and queer,
Of battles won and scents held dear.
So while they frown and seem quite stern,
Their tales bring laughter in return.

An Elegy for Flowers Yet to Bloom

In a pot where dreams are sown,
Tiny seeds sit all alone.
"I can't blossom with this gloom,
Should I just pack my bags and zoom?"

A shy bud answers with a grin,
"Why rush when you can just begin?
Patience, friend, the sun will show,
A touch of warmth and you will glow!"

The petals giggle, roots entwined,
As whispers float through space and time.
"Next week, we'll throw a grand debut,
With raindrops as our fancy dew!"

So here we sit, unbloomed but spry,
In a dance of hopes that touch the sky.
For every wait is just a chance,
To herald joy with vibrant dance!

The Way of Blossoms and Breath

In the garden of giggles, we prance,
Flowers bloom while we take a chance.
Skip along petals, pink and round,
Laughter erupts with each silly sound.

Bumblebees buzz, doing the dance,
Spreading joy with every chance.
Petals tickle our toes, what a sight,
Twirl in circles, oh what pure delight!

Sunshine giggles through the leaves,
As we dance and play like thieves.
Collecting smiles in our flowered sack,
Blossoms and breath – we won't look back!

With a wink and a playful shout,
Who knew blooms could make us pout?
Yet here we are, so light and free,
In this lovely floral jubilee!

Harvesting Aromas of Delight

In a field of scents, we run amok,
Sniffing flowers, oh what good luck!
With noses twitching, we take a dive,
Into laughter where aromas thrive.

Pollen parties, make us sneeze,
Dancing with bees, oh such a tease!
Every breeze carries sweet bouquet,
Filling our hearts, come what may!

Unruly petals stuck in our hair,
We twirl like wind, without a care.
Aromatic dreams on merry-go-round,
In this fragrant fun we are crowned!

Harvesting giggles while petals spill,
Every whiff gives us such a thrill.
So here we roam in crazy delight,
In blooms of joy, everything feels right!

Reveries in a Blossom-Covered Path

Walking the lane of joy and bloom,
Every color chases away the gloom.
With flowers giggling under the sun,
We skip and hop, oh what fun!

Petals are pillows, soft and bright,
In a world where everything feels right.
Chasing butterflies, don't let them flee,
Each flitter brings more laughter, you see!

Stumbling on blooms, making it rain,
A floral cascade, oh let's do it again!
Giggling moss in a shady nook,
With every turn, we can't help but look!

In a dreamland where silliness reigns,
Dancing to nature's sweet refrains.
With blossoms around, let troubles depart,
In a garden of giggles, we laugh from the heart!

Curved Lines of Tender Blooms

We weave through hedges with giddy delight,
Where sweetness lingers, oh what a sight!
Dandelion crowns upon our heads,
In this kingdom where laughter spreads.

Swirling petals like confetti in air,
With cheerful grins, we have not a care.
Each flower's story tickles our ears,
Blooming cartoons that chase away fears!

Counting the colors, from pink to blue,
As we run wild, we forget what's due.
Conversations with blossoms, oh my,
While butterflies giggle and flutter by!

Curved with joy, we gather and sway,
Here among blooms, where we laugh and play.
Tender moments, with smiles that loom,
In a crazy, colorful floral room!

The Soul's Journey Amidst Petals

Oh, my spirit's taking a stroll,
Through gardens that tickle my soul.
With every step, I trip on a bloom,
And dance like I'm lost in a room.

Petals whisper secrets so sweet,
While bugs join my jive with their feet.
A rose nudges me, 'Hey, don't you fall!'
I laugh as I zigzag and sprawl.

Butterflies laugh at my silly spree,
They say, "Come on, join our jubilee!"
A tulip raises its vibrant head,
"Just don't spill coffee on my bed!"

At last, I find peace in the mirth,
Among the blooms, I know my worth.
With petals on my head like a crown,
I'm the queen of this flowery town!

Threads of Color Woven in Light

In a world of threads, I'll take a chance,
Where daisies join in a wild dance.
A stitch here, a blow from the breeze,
Creating chaos with floral ease.

A daffodil says, "Pick a hue!"
I point to the one that jokes like a shoe.
"You can't wear petals, silly," it beams,
I chuckle, lost in color dreams.

The sun pours laughter like honeyed tea,
While violets giggle, "Just wait and see!"
A bluebell winks, "Can I join the fun?"
"Sure," I reply, "Let's bask in the sun!"

Now I'm wrapped in a quilt of delight,
With flowers weaving tales so bright.
Each thread a giggle, each bloom a tune,
I'm draped in color beneath the moon!

Driftwood and Dahlia Dreams

By the shore where driftwood meets flowers,
I daydream for hours and hours.
A dahlia says, "Hey, aren't you silly?"
I reply, "Only when feeling frilly!"

The sea whispers jokes to the breeze,
While daisies chuckle with teasing ease.
Driftwood sighs, "Oh, you're a real hoot!"
"Just wait until you hear my flute!"

I gather shells, crafting my crown,
With pebbles that bounce and never frown.
Each gull overhead throws down some sass,
As I trip and tumble, so full of class!

In this lively blend of wood and bloom,
I dance to the rhythm of nature's tune.
With laughter and flowers, a beautiful scheme,
My heart's adrift in these dahlia dreams!

The Symphony of Seasonal Blooms

In the spring, I called the flowers to play,
Each bloom had its song, in its own way.
The lilacs croon with a lavender tone,
While pansies join in, feeling right at home.

Summer rolls in with a trumpet so loud,
Roses sway proudly, formed like a crowd.
Sunflowers do the towering dance,
While snapdragons wait for their chance.

But autumn arrives with a flute made of leaves,
As chrysanthemums twirl, dancing in eaves.
"Don't step on my toes!" a marigold shouts,
While the pumpkins giggle, joining the bouts.

In winter, the blooms take a snooze,
While snowflakes hum with a cozy muse.
Yet deep in dreams, they plot their encore,
For next season's laughter, all ready to soar!

Nature's Tapestry Unfurled

In the garden, a bee takes flight,
Wearing shades, feeling quite bright.
Flowers giggle, sway to the beat,
Nature's dance, oh, what a treat!

Bugs in tuxedos, feeling so spry,
Chasing each other as they fly high.
A butterfly slips, lands on a hat,
'Excuse me!' it flutters, 'I'm no acrobat!'

Daffodils nod, sharing a joke,
While the oak tree chuckles, 'Oh, I'm just smoke!'
The sun sips on lemonade, feeling so fine,
As clouds play poker beneath the pines.

Thus unfolds nature's playful charade,
In this whimsical outdoor parade.
With laughter sprouting from each bloom,
Life bustles forward, dispelling the gloom.

Glimmers of Hope in Bloom

A squirrel with dreams of climbing so high,
Bounces from branches, a natural spy.
Watching the flowers, with snickers and peeks,
'Are those blooming socks or just petal peaks?'

The daisies gossip, their petals all round,
'Have you seen the rose? It's spinning around!'
'That's just the wind, she's dancing away,'
They laugh 'till they sway, come join in the fray!'

Butterflies giggle, a colorful crew,
'On Mondays we wear polka dots, it's true!'
They twirl 'round the hyacinths, full of delight,
"Who knew flowers could party all night?"

In the midst of it all, a sunflower grins,
'Let's throw a party, invite all our kin!'
With joy in the air and laughter that blooms,
Even the weeds find ways to assume groomed.

Flourishing Dreams Beneath the Sky

A robin sings with a twinkle in eye,
'Don't mind me, I'm just aiming for the sky!'
While daisies compete for the best sunny spot,
'Oh, look at me, I'm the biggest, I'm hot!'

Tulips with swagger, painted in flair,
Prancing about, they don't have a care.
'Watch out, my friends, I'm about to erupt!'
And then they sway, all proudly corrupt!

The violets murmur, 'What's that noise?'
'It's just the bees, they're full of sweet joys!'
Trotting around, they're dancing on air,
Spreading their giggles everywhere!

So come and play in this garden of cheer,
With flowers laughing from far and near.
In this realm of flutters, our hearts take flight,
Dreams blossom boldly, each day full of light.

Where Petals Meet the Ground

A ladybug winks, wearing a bow,
'Do you think I'm fancy, or just so-so?'
While the daisies compete in a beauty parade,
Claiming finest petals, all colors displayed!

With thorns for a guard and chatter so loud,
The roses boast proudly, 'We wear the crown!'
But lilacs just giggle, 'We're soft and we bloom,
Let's see who gets picked for the dance on the loom!'

The earthworms wiggle, 'Keep off the tickets!',
Hiding their stashes, the secret little snippets.
'Who can resist such a garden delight?',
While sunflowers play peek-a-boo with the light!

As petals drift gently, a colorful scene,
Each blossom insists, 'I'm the most keen!'
In a world full of laughter, oh, what a sound,
Joyfully spreading, where petals hit ground!

Petal-Laden Journeys

With a bounce in my step, I roam,
Peonies blush, guiding me home.
I tripped on a root, landed with flair,
Now bees are buzzing, I'm stuck in mid-air.

The squirrels join in, a laughter parade,
As I dance with the flowers, my worries all fade.
With petals in pockets, my pockets overflow,
Caught in their charm, I put on a show.

Chasing my dreams through a floral maze,
Each bloom a joker that sets my heart ablaze.
I hear whispered giggles from blossoms nearby,
A bouquet of cheer, oh me, oh my!

So here's to the trails where blooms giggle bright,
Where laughter and petals are pure delight.
With joy in my heart, I stick out my tongue,
In this petal-laden journey, forever I'm young.

Echoes of Blooming Hearts

In the garden of giggles, we frolic and play,
With flowers a-winking, they brighten the day.
I tripped on a daisy, oh what a sight,
The tulips all chuckle, 'Get up, take flight!'

Whispers of petals dance in the breeze,
My heart does a flip, as I trip on the leaves.
With every bright bloom, a story unfolds,
Of laughter and joy, more precious than gold.

Hey, Mr. Bumblebee, what's your plan?
You buzz with a rhythm, like a funky band.
While peonies chuckle, their colors in bloom,
I prance like a fool, let's dance to the tune!

Echoes of laughter ring soft in the air,
With petals as confetti, we float without care.
I'll slip on a leaf, but I don't really mind,
For in this garden joke, pure joy I find.

Scented Footsteps in Spring

With each scented step, I bounce down the lane,
Peonies beckon, we're all a bit insane.
I swayed with a flower, it took me for a spin,
And now I'm stuck wearing pollen like skin.

The daisies are laughing, the lilies all cheer,
My floral parade puts on a grand show here.
With bees in my hair and petals galore,
Every step that I take, makes my spirits soar.

With giggles and whispers, we frolic bold,
Through gardens of laughter, where joy can't be sold.
I accidentally rolled into a patch of mud,
But the daisies just giggle, "You look good like that, bud!"

So here in this springtime, with each fragrant breeze,
Footsteps of laughter dance with such ease.
With petals around me, I tiptoe and glide,
In a world full of flowers, I take joyful pride.

The Wayward Orchard

In an orchard of chaos, I wander with glee,
Where fruit flies are gossiping, buzzing at me.
I tried to pick apples, but swung and missed wide,
The pears laughed so hard, they fell with a slide.

Dancing with cactus, oh what a blunder,
While peaches conspired to pull off a wonder.
With shoes made of petals, I twirled with the trees,
While lemons threw shade, they acted like queens.

In this orchard of giggles, sweet fruits go awry,
An adventure unfolds, beneath a blue sky.
The cherries popped jokes, their laughter so bright,
While I stumbled and giggled, oh what a sight!

So here in the fruity, fun-filled domain,
Where vines tell my stories and laughter's my gain.
With blossoms beside me, my heart's on display,
In this wayward orchard, I dance and I sway.

The Dance of Blooming Hues

Bright blossoms sway in the breeze,
Chasing the bees like mischievous tease.
Petals pirouette, gossip with glee,
Who knew flowers could dance, oh me!

Sprightly colors in a floral fling,
The tulips laugh, the daisies sing.
Each bloom dons its fanciest gear,
Twirling and whirling, with nothing to fear.

A riot of shades, a vivid ballet,
Watching this shindig really makes my day.
Even the roses trade whispers and charms,
As they flaunt their beauty, disarming alarms.

So grab your hat, join the fun parade,
In this garden rave where worries do fade.
Let laughter blossom, it's time to imbue,
Life's more than green; it's quite the hullabaloo!

Soft Murmurs of a Flowered Trail

Along the way, blooms chatter soft,
Petals giggle, they're never too worn off.
'Hey, did you see that clumsy old bee?'
They whisper about nature's comedy spree.

Dandelions puff with a cheeky grin,
Spreading their fluff, oh where to begin?
Like tiny balloons in a cluttered sky,
They float with dreams as they pass on by.

Lavender looks chic in purple attire,
While violets play secret matchmaker's hire.
Each flower speaks, with tales thick and rich,
Who knew gardens could be such a niche?

With each petal's quirk, there's a story to tell,
In this floral adventure, everything's swell.
Nature's a jester, with beauty and cheer,
Come dance with the buds, let go of your fear!

Elysian Fields of Petal Shadows

In fields where sunlight catches the sheen,
Blooms wave hello, but what does it mean?
"Do you prefer tea or a sprinkle of rain?"
Petals gossip, not a thought of disdain.

Sunflowers stand tall, with heads held up high,
"Did you hear about that dandelion spy?"
Tales of mischief, they share with delight,
As petals quiver, it's quite the sight.

The marigolds boast of their golden hue,
While the lilacs wink at a passing blue.
"Who needs a snooze when the world's a stage?"
They giggle and tease, like flowers of age.

So wander through shadows where laughter ignites,
In the symphony of colors, the heart takes flight.
With every cheeky petal, joy will bestow,
Come walk through the garden, let the chuckles flow!

Ribbons of Color in the Sunlight

Ribbons of color stretch wide in the sun,
Floral confetti, oh, what a fun run!
"Hey, check that daisy, she's got quite the flair!"
They tease and they twirl, with flowers to share.

Petunias prank with their flashy display,
Racing with tulips, come join in the play.
The wind is a friend, oh what a delight,
It sweeps through the garden, setting warmth alight.

Chrysanthemums giggle, sharing sweet tales,
Of snails who wear jackets and dance with their sails.
"Let's throw a party, just us blooms and greens!"
In the laughter of blossoms, joy bursts at the seams.

So dive into color, let your spirit soar,
In this floral fiesta, leave your worries at the door.
For nature's a comedian, with humor to share,
In ribbons of color, find joy everywhere!

Heartbeats in a Field of Flowers

In the garden, bees do dance,
With pollen suits, they take a chance.
A ladybug in polka dots,
Looks for snacks in tangled spots.

A dandelion waves hello,
While ants march in a little row.
The sunflowers stretch just like cats,
And rabbits plot some funny chats.

A squirrel with a feeding plan,
Shares his acorns with a fan.
In nature's party, laughter rings,
As every bloom lets out their springs.

The wind, it giggles through the leaves,
Telling tales the flower weaves.
In fields where colors come alive,
Nature's humor helps us thrive.

A Glimpse into Floral Whispers

Petals gossip in the breeze,
While butterflies pretend to tease.
The daisies chuckle, 'Here we grow!'
As bees join in the funny show.

A bumblebee dropped by to chat,
Told a story, stretched on a mat.
With every buzz, a laugh unfolds,
In this kingdom, joy beholds.

A sunflower winks at the sky,
As clover plays the shy guy.
Each bloom a character distinct,
In nature's play, they're all succinct.

A tiny worm with grand designs,
Dreams of castles made of vines.
In whispers sweet, the flowers sing,
A world of joy that blooms in spring.

Caresses of Light Among the Blooms

The sunbeams tease the blooms so bright,
Whispering secrets day and night.
A rose complains about its thorns,
While nearby daisies laugh at scorns.

Butterflies don't quite use their wings,
When flowers make some funny things.
Secret meetings held at dawn,
To plan the pranks they'll pull at dawn.

A tulip flaunts its vibrant hues,
While violets share their funny views.
Each blossom wears its brightest grin,
As laughter spreads, it just begins.

What fun it is in nature's crew,
As sunlight sparks the flowers' hues.
In the garden's warm embrace,
Joy blooms here, a happy place.

Vistas of Floral Harmony

A canvas rich with colors bold,
Where laughter blooms and joy unfolds.
The poppies pop and winks they share,
As bumblebees float in the air.

A twist of petals, a giggle bright,
The floral friends bask in the light.
Each bloom a joker, skilled, sublime,
Tickling the world with rhythm and rhyme.

The violets throw a silly dance,
As honeybees take a crazy chance.
With roots entwined, they form a band,
Playing jokes across the land.

From tulip's smile to rose's cheek,
The blooms share laughter, oh so sweet.
In vistas wide where joy takes hold,
The flowers tell tales of bright and bold.

Sylphs Among Silken Ribbons

In the garden where giggles play,
Sylphs dance with ribbons, oh what a sway!
They trip on their toes, not quite in grace,
Twirling like tops, in a comical race.

They whisper to blooms, 'Do you see that bee?'
Who buzzes around, drunk on sweet tea.
But off he flies, with a shimmy and shake,
Leaving poor sylphs to giggle and quake.

A petal parade in the soft morning light,
Each blossom tells jokes, oh what a sight!
With pranks played on squirrels, and laughs in between,
Nature's own jesters, a comical scene.

So if you should wander, don't be so grim,
Join the dance party, just follow the whim.
For life in the garden, with every hooray,
Is laughter and joy, in a sprightly ballet.

Luminescent Blossoms at Twilight

When twilight arrives, and the sky wears a grin,
The blossoms ignite, like they're hosting a din.
Each petal a lantern, it's quite the display,
While ants on the ground plan a dance in ballet.

They gather and chatter, with secrets to share,
Whispers of pollen, in the cool evening air.
"Oh look at that moon, it's just like a pie!"
They giggle and nudge as the fireflies fly.

Bumblebees stutter their sweet little hums,
Confused by the light, they bump like clumsy bums.
With petals that shimmer, a waltz takes its claim,
Made brighter by laughter, that's part of the game.

So under the stars, in their revelry bright,
The blooms throw a party, each night's such a sight.
It's a floral fiesta, with joy all around,
As we dance with the blossoms, lost in the sound.

Swaying on Gentle Winds

In a field where the breezes like to frolic and tease,
The flowers take turns to twirl with such ease.
"I'll lead," says the daisy, with a twist and a twirl,
While the tulip just giggles and gives a swift whirl.

"Watch out for the dandelions," the daisies all warn,
"They scatter their fluff like a sudden spring storm!"
And so they all dance, in a whimsical chase,
While the sun spills his laughter, flooding the space.

With shadows that shiver, the petals do leap,
The chives wear their hats, looking silly, not cheap.
A chorus of colors, a comedy show,
Where the blooms all unite in a cheerful tableau.

As dusk paints the sky with a palette of dream,
The flowers still sway, in a whimsical stream.
For when the wind blows, they giggle and play,
In a garden of humor, come join or delay!

Mosaic of Nature's Canvas

On nature's grand canvas, colors splash bright,
With giggles of flowers, a whimsical sight.
The roses declare, "We've got such a flair!"
While humble old weeds just shrug with despair.

A sunflower jests, "I'm the king of this plot!
With my tall golden head and a smile oh so rot!"
But a clover nearby rolls its eyes in disdain,
And nudges the daisies, saying, "Isn't he vain?"

The marigolds chuckle, their blooms all in sync,
"Let's paint this whole garden with laughter, don't you think?"
Each petal a burst of humor and cheer,
As they find their own comical rhythm right here.

So gather, dear friends, at this playful show,
Where whimsy reigns free and the laughter will flow.
For in this grand tapestry, colors combine,
Creating a mosaic where blooms intertwine.

Blossoms in the Breeze

In gardens bright where petals swirl,
The bumblebee does quite the twirl.
A clumsy dance, a fuzzy sight,
He steals my snacks, then takes to flight.

With every gust, the flowers sway,
A kite gone rogue, they fly away.
I chase them down, in joy I bound,
While giggling blooms all around.

Trails of Fragrant Dreams

There's a trail where scents collide,
With roses laughing, side by side.
A daisy jokes, a tulip grins,
While sneaky ants plan where to begin.

The daisies dabbed with dew so sly,
Propose a feast, and oh my, oh my!
They served us pie, but it was tough,
I laughed so hard, I'd had enough!

Garden Whispers at Dusk

As dusk descends, the flowers chat,
The lilies gossip 'bout this and that.
'Which butterfly has most flair?'
The peonies shout, 'We don't care!'

The hedgehog strolls, with puzzled mien,
Interrupts the gossipers, quite obscene.
'Are you all snug, or just a show?'
They giggle, 'Hedgehog, you really don't know?'

The Color of Serendipity

In hues of pink and yellow hues,
The petals tease their morning snooze.
A splash of laughter, a dash of glee,
Mixed with the bees' sweet symphony.

They played a game of hide and seek,
While flower crowns made noses peak.
Each bloom a jester, light and bright,
With pollen jokes that take the cake tonight!

Melodies Among Swaying Stems

Bobby danced with pots in tow,
A flower crown, he stole the show.
The bees all buzzed a serenade,
While petals rained, a colorful parade.

He twirled and slipped in petals bright,
A slip of fate, what a sight!
The tulips giggled, chuckling loud,
As Bobby bowed, feeling proud.

A bee named Rick yelled, "Hey, cool guy!"
"Why not join us? Don't be shy!"
Together, they swayed, a madcap crew,
A merry jig under skies so blue.

With laughter ringing, they spun around,
Making merry with the flowers found.
Bobby left with pollen in his hair,
A jester's title, he'd gladly wear.

Ephemeral Trail of Floral Dreams

In a field where colors dance and sway,
Lucy lost her hat one day.
A daisy smiled, 'Here, take my bloom!'
While tulips giggled, filling the room.

Her dreams were wild, her dress awry,
A bouquet fashioned, oh my, oh my!
With every step, she left a trace,
Of petals bright in a funny chase.

The daisies laughed, 'She's off her game!"
"Should we tell her? No, let's play!"
As she twirled, a clumsy queen,
In a floral realm, the funniest scene.

As butterflies cheered with wings outspread,
Lucy spun with flowers for a crown on her head.
With joy, she hums a silly tune,
Underneath the bright, whimsical moon.

Celestial Blossom Constellations

Stars fell down in a flowery heap,
While lily pads held a secret to keep.
Edgar, the cat, with a twinkle in eye,
Juggled daisies, passing them by.

Onlookers gasped, it was such a sight,
As Edgar danced under the moonlight.
A daffodil yelled, "You've got no grace!"
Edgar winked, "I'm winning this race!"

The stars above began to sway,
In laughter and joy, they joined the play.
With every pounce and every spin,
Edgar thought he could finally win.

Yet petals surrounded him, in piles so high,
He tripped and tumbled, oh my, oh my!
In the blossoms, he found a cozy bed,
The funny cat with dreams in his head.

Journey Through Hues of Twilight

On a twilight stroll, the colors amazed,
Charlie the turtle was slightly dazed.
"Is that a peony or a sunny chair?"
He sighed, as the twilight glared.

The sky turned orange, then pink in a flash,
"Why walk when I can roll? Dash, dash!"
The daisies laughed, "Come join the game!"
As Charlie rolled, he earned his fame.

With each little bump, a laugh did unfold,
"I'm winning this race!" he boldly told.
But round and round he went in delight,
A merry chase till he lost the light.

A tulip cried out, "Oh look, he's stuck!"
"Should we help or just wish him luck?"
In the colors of twilight, what a fun scene,
As Charlie chuckled, 'I'm living the dream!'

Vibrant Stories Beneath the Canopy

A squirrel stole my sandwich today,
He danced like he knew it was play!
Between the lush leaves, a giggle in air,
I yelled, 'Hey buddy! Some manners, I swear!'

The flowers laughed as the breeze went by,
Waving their petals, as if to comply.
"Stealing is wrong, don't you think so?"
The proud little bud gave the nut thief a show.

The plants chimed in, in a rustling cheer,
"We need a committee, so gather near!"
With petals for hats and roots tangled tight,
They set up a court, all things felt right!

And so in the shade, we had our own law,
With blossoms as judges and grass as a floor.
The squirrel, still snacking, just winked with glee,
He left me to ponder, "Was it justice or tea?"

The Essence of Delicate Days

Oh dear, what's that? A flying bee,
Did it just take a liking to me?
With a buzz and a zig, it darted on quick,
Might I be the next floral trick?

A ladybug strolls with a grand little strut,
While ants make a line in a garden hut.
"Excuse me," I said, "You're stepping on grains!"
But they just kept marching, in petal-like trains.

The tulips just chuckle, they shake in delight,
As petals get tangled in pure garden flight.
"It's dance day!" they sing with unbridled thrill,
While daisies conga with time to kill!

So here in this green, with all of my friends,
We laugh and we twirl, where the fun never ends.
For life in the blooms is a whimsical game,
With laughter and sunshine, never the same!

Harmonies of the Garden Path

A snail takes a stroll, but at such a slow pace,
He declared, "I'm enjoying my race!"
While crickets all chirp an off-key refrain,
"Is that really singing, or just a disdain?"

The flowers nod off, in bright sunny glee,
"Each note is a gift, from nature, you see?
Even weeds have their say, though they're not much in style,"
They bloom with a flourish, showing off their wild.

A butterfly winks, flaunting colors so bright,
It twirls through the air, a marvelous sight.
"Balancing life is more than a task,
Just remember to smile, it's all we can ask."

With daisies in crowns and petals to spare,
They dance through the garden without a care.
The laughter flows freely, like a soft summer breeze,
In this whimsical realm, we're all here to tease!

Exquisite Blooms Under the Haze

In a patch of blooms, we tried to play hide,
But a bee took the lead, with nowhere to glide!
"Oh no, I'm the queen!" buzzed a bee with a flare,
As petals just giggled, hanging in air.

The lavender whispered, "Come smell me right here!"
"Is it spice or a prank?" asked a rose with a sneer.
"No pranks allowed, we are classy and chic!"
But the daisies popped up with their own little peek!

"Let's make a bouquet, but with silly things,
With feathers, and glitter, and sparkly rings!"
Roses turned redder, with envy galore,
"Don't make me join in, I'm far too demure!"

Yet, laughter erupted, for none could resist,
And soon the whole garden was caught in the twist.
With petals adorned in extravagant style,
Under the haze, we danced for a while!

Patterns of Nature's Palette

In the garden where colors collide,
Bees wear tiny hats, filled with pride.
Butterflies giggle, dancing on air,
Winking at flowers with nothing to wear.

Roses wear red, like a clown's big nose,
Sunflowers peek out, like a friend who knows.
Tulips do a jig, swaying with glee,
Nature's a party—come join the spree!

Daisies play poker, winning the bets,
While the daisies tell stories, forgetting their pets.
Violets tease pansies, making them laugh,
In this lively garden, there's no room for gruff.

So grab your paints, let's splash and create,
Nature's a canvas, let's open the gate.
Colorful fun, all around we see,
Join in the laughter, be wild and free!

Revelations Beneath the Blooming Skies

Under blooming skies, clouds drift in a haze,
Birds in tuxedos perform in a daze.
The sun plays tricks, tickling the flowers,
While laughter erupts for hours and hours.

A chubby squirrel, with acorns galore,
Thought he was rich, now he's quite poor.
He lost his stash, but found a lost shoe,
Squeezing his feet, he laughs, 'Who knew?'

Petals gossip softly, whispers abound,
Spiders in top hats, spinning around.
Each bloom unfolds, revealing a jest,
With secrets and laughs, it's nature's best fest.

So gaze at the sky, let laughter take flight,
Embrace the whimsy, from morning 'til night.
Every leaf giggles, life's moments ignite,
Under this bloom, everything feels right!

The Scented Echo of a Journey

On a road scented sweet, with flowers that sway,
A snail on a mission moves slowly away.
With his home on his back, he's ready to roam,
Echoing laughter, he's far from his home.

The daisies shout, 'Race ya to the stream!'
While tulips insist on a leisurely dream.
Each petal a whisper, secrets they share,
In this fragrant journey, we haven't a care.

With scents of adventure that tickle the nose,
A butterfly slips, in her graceful clothes.
She flutters and flops, takes a wild chance,
Falling in petals, joins in the dance.

So let's follow the scents, let our spirits run,
In this whimsical world, laughter's begun.
Every step blooms with joy, every twist in the flair,
The echoes of humor linger in the air!

Footprints in a Blossom-Covered Land

In a land where flowers bloom wide and bright,
A toddler tiptoes, laughing with delight.
Each step is a squish, through colors galore,
'Oops! I just painted!' he shouts with a roar.

The petals lead on, like a mischievous path,
Where ants host a picnic, evoking a laugh.
Ladybugs dance, and bees join the fun,
In this silly garden, there's laughs for everyone.

With footprints of laughter, bright splashes of hue,
Every step taken brings giggles anew.
The blossoms are witnesses, keeping the score,
As children play tag—who could ask for more?

So wander this land, where each flower's a friend,
In the blossom's embrace, let your worries suspend.
With every fun step, let the giggles expand,
In this joyous journey, through blossoms we stand!

www.ingramcontent.com/pod-product-compliance
Lightning Source LLC
Chambersburg PA
CBHW071813160426
43209CB00003B/76